From Apple to Zipper

by Nora Cohen

illustrated by Donna Kern

Aladdin Books
Macmillan Publishing Company   New York
Maxwell Macmillan Canada   Toronto
Maxwell Macmillan International   New York   Oxford   Singapore   Sydney

A is for

pple

with a bite from its side.

B is for

BOX

with its flaps opened wide.

C is for

Crayon

to draw and to write.

D is for

D iamond

so sparkling and bright.

E is for **Egg**

to scramble or fry.

F

is for

lag

it waves in the sky.

G is for

Goldfish

who glides through the sea.

H

is for

ouse

warm and cozy for me.

I

I is for

ce cubes

stacked up so tall.

J is for

Jacks

with a bouncing red ball.

K is for

Keys

both modern and old.

L is for Lobster so orange and bold.

M is for

Maze

and a mouse who is hasty.

N is for Noodles

so golden and tasty.

O is for

Orange

with a hole in the middle.

P is for

encil

to write down a riddle.

Q is for **Q**uilt

to warm up my toes.

R is for

Ribbon

to tie into bows.

S is for
ea
horse

through water it's gliding.

T is for

Tree

for climbing and hiding.

U is for

mbrella

it shields me from showers.

V is for Vase

to fill with fresh flowers.

W is for **W**aves rolling onto the sand.

X is for **X**ylophone

to play in the band.

Y Y Y Y Y Y Y

Y **Y** is for

Y arn

with needles to knit.

Y Y Y Y Y Y Y

Z is for **Z**ipper

it's just the right fit.

First Aladdin Books edition 1993
Text copyright ©1993 by Nora Cohen
Illustrations copyright ©1989, 1993 by Donna Kern
Poster copyright ©1989, 1993 by Donna Kern

Aladdin Books
Macmillan Publishing Company
866 Third Avenue
New York, NY 10022

Maxwell Macmillan Canada
1200 Eglinton Avenue East
Suite 200
Don Mills, Ontario M3C 3N1

Macmillan Publishing Company is part of the Maxwell Communication Group of Companies.

Printed in the United States of America
Book design by Chani Yammer

10   2 1

Library of Congress Cataloging-in-Publication Data
Tarlow, Nora. From apple to zipper / Nora Cohen; illustrated by Donna Kern.
        — 1st Aladdin Books ed.
                p.   cm.
Summary: Includes rhyming text with words illustrated from the letters they represent.

1. English language — Alphabet — Juvenile literature.
2. Alphabet rhymes. [1. Alphabet.] I. Kern, Donna, ill.   II. Title.
                        PE1155.
        [E]—dc20   92-43691